The Weave

Thurston Moore, known as founder of Sonic Youth, avant-garde NYC noise rock group from 1981–2014, is editor of *Ecstatic Peace Poetry Journal*, author of *Alabama Wildman* (Water Row USA), *Stereo Sanctity* (Ecstatic Peace Library USA) and many other books of writing. He currently resides in London as a musician, publisher of Ecstatic Peace Library, and teaches at the RMC in Copenhagen and the Jack Kerouac School of Disembodied Poetics at Naropa University, Boulder Colorado.

John Kinsella is the author of over forty books. His many awards include the Australian Prime Minister's Literary Award for Poetry. His most recent works include the poetry volumes *Drowning in Wheat: Selected Poems* (Picador, 2016) and *Open Door* (UWAP, 2018). He often works in collaboration with other poets, artists, musicians, and activists. He is a Fellow of Churchill College, Cambridge University, and Professor of Literature and Environment at Curtin University, Western Australia. He lives on Ballardong Noongar land at Jam Tree Gully in the Western Australian wheatbelt. In 2007 he received the Christopher Brennan Award for Lifetime Achievement in Poetry.

The Weave

THURSTON MOORE
& JOHN KINSELLA

First published in 2020 by
UWA Publishing
Crawley, Western Australia 6009
www.uwap.uwa.edu.au

UWAP is an imprint of UWA Publishing,
a division of The University of Western Australia.

ISBN: 978-1-76080-135-9

A catalogue record for this book is available from the National Library of Australia

Cover design by Alissa Dinallo
Typeset by Lasertype
Printed by Lightning Source

Contents

Buzzkill 7
Scarabs 9

A REMARKABLE GREY HORSE 11
Skeleton Key 13
Double-Glazed 14
Rounding the Point 17
Tout (or Scalper) 21
Skateboard 23
Ode to Doris Day 24
Zesty 25
Luis Buñuel's Day Off 26
Blow: A Sonnet 29
Mattress 30
Rimbaud was Addicted to Television 32

POST-HORSE 33
Trash Frost Ghost Saint Lullaby 35
Ramshine 38

SWITCHED ON 39

STREET PARTY 61
Lightkick! 63
Lightkick! 2 71
Lightkick! 3 74
Psych-brat [*] 76
Linethrow all breve 77
Signal Jamming 82
Helix Unfurled 85
jazz junk makes freedom
(thinking of wyatt) 87
Hunkydory 88
Criss-cross 91
Photo-finish 94

Interview by Rosie Long Decter 95

Acknowledgements 109

Buzzkill

In the constant tramline motion of his trainers
He took the third and added a choice amendment
To their wish fulfilment; but don't doubt he loved –

He did, big time and strong, the tall buildings wavering.
Sneaker rocker ripping holes in the velvet sky
Beards howl hoot spurt in any/all directions

Celebrate dystopia and delirious freefall!
Knock, come in, close curtain, breathe, slap
And tickle your way – his way – to joyous

Occasional relapse. We are all too fallible,
He noted, riding high on subway vapours, trapping
Phonemes from their speech bubbles, making

Debauched art in the depths of his positronic
Spectacle of sound and deathwish. Drag him
Out of bed, straddle him and know the mosaic

Is riddled with grace and temptation, take a leaf,
Take his better judgement, and heap praise on his
View Down Town – those ticket stubs of pleasure,

those cars stacked high as pheromones;
those lads with eyes on buttercream girls;
those idols with sonic points of reference;

those wizards who sense the coming collision;
those wisps that excite the heart, music spreading gold;
those clotted needles in trash cans searched out again;

Remixing the mess of his days, he checks out of the city
And makes itinerant on country roads, a crossroads
Judgement, a falling in with good ol' boys
    Who'll take him down.

Scarabs

Ah let's do new where scarabs click
Resonant dust from hashish headlight
Forever dream thing sweeps through high brocade
And mind is central, serene, lavender mists

With a sucker punch below the graft,
Below a mortar and pestle imprimatur –
Those long licks, those trance flings,
That flash of dry out of the wet;

Remove the quotes and flounce to sun ship
Kingdoms crashing hard with strange assonance,
Ululations distorted by deep rattle, O and
Spoiled silence languishing in its rowdy pleasure.

That's what left us to our own resources,
To that megaplex of realisation: mode of transport,
Hub of communication, a brutal parrot flying low,
All shadowed in our pastoral no-show.

Pataphysic pill reappears in soft library
Love tongue slips into life time masque
Darby Crash and pals' push-down-mohawk
Upending trash cans and prepare for (death)(happiness)

And so say all of us, hustled and hoarded,
ridden into the dirt. An echo of track success
grates their nerves and we take a collection
from what's left – misfire, undertaker, less worthy.

A REMARKABLE GREY HORSE

Skeleton Key

Foundry time flakes the keyhole
layers a mascara settlement,
takes Julia to the cleaners

This is our new nude noise
Jazz begins in the flurry
The skin of a thousand moments

as we take in our last sights,
hold Liberty's torch up Dignity's
lurching personifications.

Double-Glazed

Through the double-glaze the village warps,
an abreaction to Halloween hangovers,
the ghosts busy about garbage disposals

Oh dear that light is burning so very false
Can we shut the pseudo-aluminum sickness (please)
Dear real heart make love make love
You and you on our couch

Yes, yes, I hear Anaïs speaking to Henry,
I catch the sun on the curtains
making summertime as winter comes on,
I hear ice clawing at the pipes

No sugar! Time for action
Is imperfectly now. This pre-dawn
We splash! Paint! (Poems!) on evil market
Displacement
        of social sense
                by scummed skullduggery

Relapsing into cartoons and undercoats,
testaments and bewailings, a cost-
cutting measure in oldtown cul-de-sacs

She works for a world of soul
Power in the knowledge, the purpose
Of grace. Her punk kid fights
        for her freedom
            our incandescence

Taking stock, nouveau Money Bags
and his vibrant entourage
switched allegiance to offshore
arms companies: yachts on the harbour

So a bow to silence, the dark silver
Winter late noon and sacrifice
The judges know naught of our embrace
Our state of delight

Rounding the Point

Rounding the point in heavy weather
they aim for the harbour, corkscrewing
hope and good fortune, a lighthouse
giving out ribbons of darkness

Grease on water slick black
The wet eyes, skin bathed in heat
Let the air in * break the window
Open / flights to the cinema are tonight
and tomorrow morning :
the improviser's (!!!... sexplosion)
--::-- *
J
O
Y

jouissance
omnipresent
yearning
lifting the hand from the tiller,
taken as a suggestive, a grammar
overload and trimming the sheets,

stained but who gives a damn
*--::--

I believe in all things invisible
Because because
Yr words have incredible stink I love you
Lighthouse lovers unite light
House light lover w/ ribbons round
Yr waist

sucked off by an anemone
the lighthouse gives nothing back
but we make our own pleasure
waves breaking over the bow

I command you to sleep
and to forget me – but hold
close – the gulls sounding –
Pure message, sight, grace

in the full fathom five,
the snakes alive, the mouth
to mouth passage of seawater,
a limpet's refusal to stick

Green is the colour of
my true loves hair, the siren
of sonar life, burbling undercover
from the landlubber's gunk
Yr majesty, the mystery

Rounding the point in heavy weather
they aim for the harbour, corkscrewing
hope and good fortune, a lighthouse
giving out ribbons of darkness

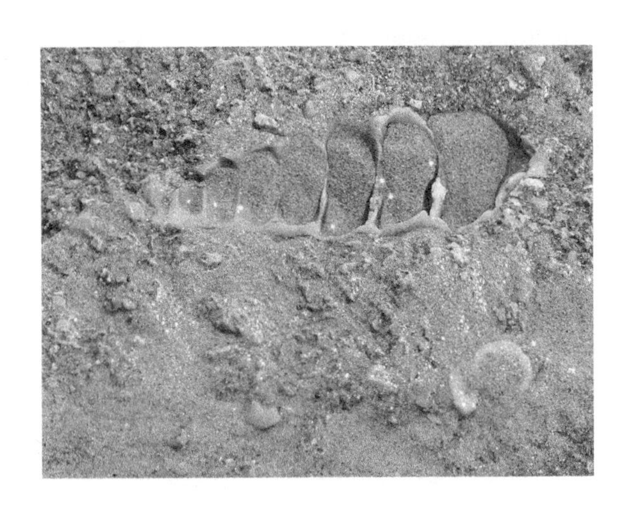

Tout (or Scalper)

Skimming underworld testaments
as we dive a garment taste-test,
value-adding sampled talent,
lest we forget in endless queues;

You were a no-show at the club
Killing it in the studio
THAT energy is where dreams
Live to tell (the transcripts a mist)
Blood

        conserves a wealthy
blast of presence, conditioning
a leisurely stroll across
the screen, a shadowplay
or massacre

...Perfect landing dear mind destroyer!
Shall we bust a few brews for the punks
    on parade (in pyjamas and shades of
        sick chartreuse) for the delight
            of nightmare rock n roll??

Yeah, why not; mohawks
bobbing into the ceiling fan,
cut down to dye-slick and stubble,
pinpoints of a planetarium,
cosmic needle-stick

Water damage scree we slash
the tyres of fattened
fobs intent on exclusive spume,
Their lips glossed by its skuzz
diapers damp with entitlements turds

I mean, you've gotta stand your ground,
take dehydration to the crowd, touch-up
a foible, rise to take the verbals,
highkick your walking shoes,
take a hike, that dive

Now that s/he has yr number
texts and email muck will lash
yr window, striations of unctuous
info, we. are. out.

Skateboard

I skateboard up through the Guggenheim
because it is harder to take on board
Italian futurism which is hidden
in the rush

Subsequently Peggy sued me for bucks
I know I no have. Why is everyone so
sad, strident and stuck?
Your oils are glacier still, ex-
otic / mordant and…
… (new
wave) green

        and glass
dogs my every step, that clash
of civilities, a grating
of NYCTS manhole covers,
a splurge of sunrise
failing to appear with-
in me

Ode to Doris Day

That wicked wink takes the cake,
a gleam to write home about,
que sera sera, pretty as a foxeye,
the rich mix undoes the floorplan,
a chunky shoulder to rest upon

Some things one may not fuck with
and this, dear, is such, the almost
frightening cheer and brandy-lipped
will to survive, wantonly, wickedly
and with the horny hedonist's secret
of complete control

Over the Phaedrus kiss, the lippy
act of love, a surface recreation
to earth a high-flyer, a hair set
platitude to take the wind from sales,
to leave late shoppers empty-handed

Freezing my feelings for the blood
as every cell pleads
Eyes to windows where no outside "is"
Go. – close it – Go.
go

Zesty

Infra dig our surplus
harmonies, a catechism
of trance and concrete,
a howl that barely
gathers pace
out of the subway,
limps into the trash

Countless love affairs in substrata
dwellings, mice and newspapers
scatter and sweep in a harmony
in cold wind tunnel punk rock licking

to trace a thrashing, to loose
the squelch of lipgloss, coalesce
about the megaphone. We take
I to the cleaners
and nag anatomies
to break their lines.

Luis Buñuel's Day Off

Wrapping the bride in serenity and peace
(nodding off during the beggar's banquet),
He took to the screen in sweet release
(sing song zarzuela spinning on parquet).

Some sounds we hear for survival
Calming agents, restive serenades
Film reels whirl, magnetic tape on
sex head.

        Anthand, eyesplit, daybeauty
Flowering magicbox entrepreneur,
Risk assessment to needs meet,
Idle hands the Devil's bag
Of tricks.

Fingertips anoint the ageless cathedral
Its pews resonant with deep oils
Dripping voices, prayers like spume
Cosmologies on languid thighs, breath-
taking, perfect time

In a five-walled room with twin ceilings,
Lava lamps growing into the linoleum,
Uncle took to the waterbed, concealing
His scalpel in that godless praesidium.

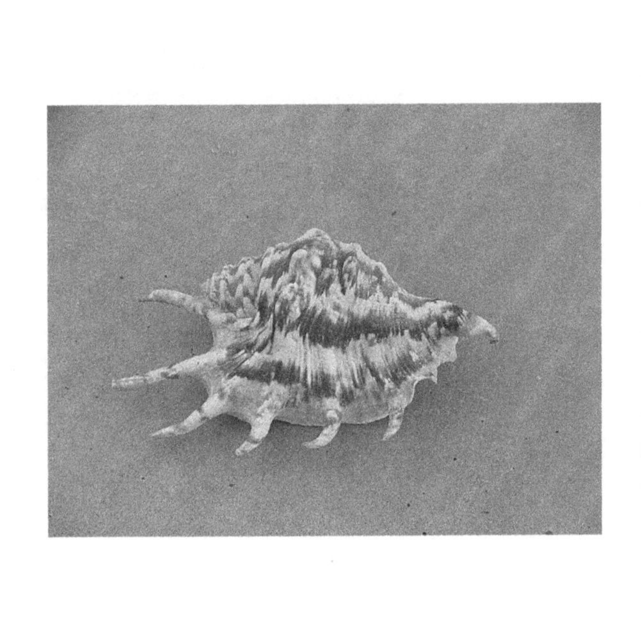

Blow: A Sonnet

Follow, follow, insane love is aching, steps, steps
To bloodtest wedding plans as this prenup sidesteps
Youth giggling dumb and unaware, pull my coat tighter
To prep the urge, caress my exit from Brooklyn; defer
Awake to see your eyes catch mine, a stroke of life
In preservative, a tour via the piazza's strife,
Crying babies, mothers, men as streetcars promise
    timelessness
Though we track down and cauterise that *locus ameonus*,
Brushed against you the vibration informing the
    meta-secret –
A tribunal of skinfold and spit-test, requisite
Keys fall from windows into lovers pockets the wars of fools
To book ten minutes of Katherine Anne's ridicule:
Trapped yet free to age as every life must
Reject its serotype and explore disgust.

Mattress

Vanished, slipping into view, re-
discurse, ink stain and rag
His head in spilt wine, eyes seek
a key to jazz collector's mattress.

Or dipping into the mute,
he surfaces a locomotive mirror,
a stash of gramophone memories
shoehorned into the archive.

spin round husband unpossessed
no lies boys they have their say
the kids creep out the grass is
going to save yr mind from sick dicklessness

or fixity in pet cemeteries, dank
Painted Ladies, floor show fecklessness,
emblazoned strikes against retina-
overload, detached from banter

perfect irrational thunk patrol
slamming in pits of future non-specificity
the hyper-jabble will go down like a mickey
licorice whips and we smile pained,

exhausted in love ok with God's dream
and junkbond perpetuity, over-
whelmed with Sturm und Drang
blasts from back catalogues.

Rimbaud was Addicted to Television

Mascara action to the four corners,
quarrymen with chips on shoulders

white cum a silver lion dripping
Beatle Paul has teeth of steel

Curtains up, angel faints from cloud
Jack the trickster ripping sky junk

to make a payload bonanza, inflationary
stooge-wreckage to traumatise arrhythmia.

POST-HORSE

Trash Frost Ghost Saint Lullaby

Trash ghosts merge wasp galls
On lanky armed wattle tree
Far from city's inversion layer

Jack in the box
Hales dead halo
Lush about plush lips

Free frost flits like saint hair
Purses snatched by lips soiled
I lick your itch ok
Wonderful meeting

To flesh out & test
Centipede reflex
Or mess with fleeting
Invectives, love's prospect

Whip it on me goldboy
First thought is predestined desire
You know
Nothing was (sun always s/peaking)

Trucked across wastes
Nothing was gross as the moon
So we hailed
The lost to rise up & come to us

Off to bed
Blues heart the reminder
All is
OK

Ramshine

Rising on the kraken wave,
a hulahoop of a break,
the skaters set their low-
riders for a sunset dip,
a slip into smooth lingo;

Lowerlips bad mouth kissing
cigs, eyes skipping pavement
honey, wild time may last
only so long, but who dares
Care? Time to slip through.

SWITCHED ON

Switched on I remark hotly
The blank headjob takes too much
Pace out of the eyelid-drop
Of stock loss and golf courses

What hope to rise in the crowd
To screeds of blanked spirit
While in the wobbling tower
Hogs snuffling know love

Like no clown warrior con artist
Boisterous as a militarized turnpike,
Such lozenges of news we take
Pill-like in the liftshaft,

Seemingly, in sniffle scuzz, does
The stagecraft swing round to court
The crowd, does the AA meeting
Rename the higher power

Power to the alms taker
Power to the junk bondage maker
Power to the skyscraper snorter
Power to the solid state e-racketeer

For she may bring new hello
For she may rewire our hungry clothes dryers
For she may call out the brown falcon striking the robin
For she may neglect to take up those carbon credits

So where do we go sans a fairground bonanza,
Light streaming out from laughing hearts
Where the crazy mirrors kill off the college kids
Drawing yet more freshers to their clown-doom

And to the goddess Marie
And her silicon valleys, her Bangalore
Toxicity of progress, the lake burning
Untreated shit from industries of communication

Eloquent in the field of charity
Lost in the field of perfection
Foaming in the run-offs, a chemical weed
Draping like viscera across the windscreen

Ravishing looks of grace and intellect
And sewage, O gigantic water lilies
We wish upon. And so from his tower
Far be it from any man to regulate

Her providence, her look down from
The fetishes he wishes upon her;
Forever and a day
Power to the steeple

Risen fabulous in overflow
We eye the king's eyepiece
Ready to run riot
Ready to intrigue our children

Ready to raise hell in the gardens
Ready to embrace the influx
Ready to ferment and foment
Ready to repeat ourselves

Tracking growth spurts
Through the portholes of bathyspheres,
The shit deep shit in the trenches
Generating its own light which doesn't rate

Being called ghostly or eerie.
Where did we turn on a pinhead?
Where did we stretch the phrase to break
The note? A photo on the hop, a photo on

The barbeque messenger board
Double-edged with fiscal charrings
And Little Lucifer Firelighters?
Or just a plain old passport photo

And biometric tell-tale sign which
States an opening in the field
Of tongue-tastic transcendence
Which means I'm outta here

Which means I am through with
Surveillance in the green room,
Which means I will grasp as straws
To poll a less-than-respectful outcome,

Which means the sewers and you all
Thinking so much less of me, vanishing
from sight, vanishing into the Zephyr's
crass valise, the mildew in its zippered pockets.

*

New lines began to emerge into a quasar reality –
First thought was age and tropoelastin and spandex
Tossed in the pot of retrospect, the big screen
Locking onto a renewed desire for surfactants,

For raking in the memories and relabelling nostalgia as
Second mortality, as a cavalcade of bunting and brass,
Bold Hogs and skateboards with invisible wheels –
And on three we charged the doors, slick as ice.

Everyone saw it coming. Everyone turned over a new leaf.
Fate is in a pleasant mood, we quipped, but our shrinking
Capacities fooled no one and we grew slightly afraid
On the pavement, a haunted look mirroring our desire.

Seriously, what's to come of it? How should we proceed?
In awe of circumstance and bakelite switch flashbacks?
Rambling in search of leftover confetti, the wasted
    bridges?
We've come to pray for jazz but have muffled our virtues.

So what of the revisions, the emollients they deploy
To work over the earth's skin, the submariners'
    apostrophes
To the light of day? Where the ministrations circle
And resolve the dark we complicate the stretch of fabrics,

We loosen lips to love the ships from stern to bow,
Taking the treadmill sunset with sealegs and scuba faith.
Who will surface to take the cake, the fallout frosting?
Who will stay up late and watch us fall to sleep?

*

New lines began to merge begin to blindside novices
to emerge First thought was a testament to samizdat in an
age Second mortality; And on a countdown to
Armageddon
three we charged the doorprice to take leave of senses –

doors of expressionist laugh-a-minutes, jests, of killjoy
facts.
Everyone saw it arriving in through but taking no blasé
ballast
coming Fate in punnets of blastdoor resonance, those
miniscule
pleasant mood capsules, those grainy replays of the first
moon landing.

In circumstance of awe we drop-jawed the final thirty
seconds!
We've come to jazz for pray and stay, for quicksliver
change but want to gain.
Where the circle ministrates a for cash only deal, we
dance a treat. Crazy mirrors.
And the dark resolves a diving bell's quartz windows
– *the Summer of Love* –

my vote on tenterhooks, vulnerable as the cable we
    suspend by,
not getting in here as advocates for barnstorming drive-
    thru services,
light dissolves yr force and a countermelody releases our
    desire for bebop;
we love the trans we love the shifts we love the fluidity we
    love the multiphonics unrestrained – so!

all stand! and sit! and roll and groove and writhe and
    levitate and reach!!
Reach out highhat and follow the signs: *Sed fugit interea,*
    fugit inreparabile tempus,
just to take a leaf as new kids finger used LPs hoping
    against hope that they'll be in the store tomorrow,
blue eyes black skins white hearts rainbow articulations
    brown eyes fair skins red hearts chromatic praises

bleed slow in safe porous genius to love with gusto
to share across all self-definitions to engage in download
magic act always welcoming always coming up
for air syncopating like presence has to be there, waiting
incorruptible.

*

Bad is not an animal word it is a transformative georgic
crush of pseudonyms it is the beast sans libido
It is an ego drive stinking of slam dunk skater
lipservice rivalry caustic hesitation on the rim of
the sump –
Slam shut putrid curtain to ribald a gloating mike-
stand hawker raddling crowd surfer interference
Rank with candy gunk and wave stress delirium in
windrow hustle to unjam picture hook bravado: let
loose!

Picket sign tattoos rock pets to betterment a blast of
testglands, a bucket on the fringe, a roadie rack
& pinion
Star versus rock star reverb to bar-write a ditty for
lovely shady impresarios who will gorge stadia as
exterminator breath
Opulence stinks the room of signings and cover
besmirches in a haunting hack of sad interfaces,
a sack of tower
Crap astounding Tangier memories or off-loading
transparent plastic cushions in the steelwork's
headoffice –

Who thinks to own the sunrise when workers choke and
 coagulate and matchstick forests fall in glory pics,
And where is protest tv and where is the filtered
 appeal of boosted semaphore on the law lawn the
 valedictory
Kali Yuga I kick with promise wanting its hope and yet
 and yet taking a fall on the curled carpet's edge of
 New Deal
Punk rock mule in ripped poverty uploading all that
 hack as fast as highspeed really is this sacred hope
 for the sacred

Beneath it all;
Ho Ho Ho disambiguation
In copyright anonymity
wherein exploits of
Justice (is) imperfect
when spelled out of *it*?

*

The incongruity of emotion
cosine western bellbird
in the magnetic mime –

The divinity of time
as loveloss promotional
primetime crime, always –

No one gets out but all
gathering about the gargoyle poet's
Prose-Verse-Poster-Algebraic-

Sym-Bolico-Riddle
Musicopoematographoscope
& Pocket Musicopoematographoscope –

Are equally to blame
in offsetting the devil
may care to wig out –

And set afire, laughing all the way
to brashfills & bronzewings so shy
as to vanish with a clause.

STREET PARTY

Lightkick!

Tremolo is no blow to circuitry of park fusion in the *mixfit* –
let's join the hullabaloo of cellular action, the photosynthesis
of alarms and alerts, the triggered mountains and ranges
of earth bell soundings – deep as data-mines caving
in on syncopation: stand up and be counted down by
worshippers?

Swans bite, they say, The bastards'
imperialist forms, gorgeous, bloodyminded
we watch and counter the truth of nature
as it cares not a whit betwixt survival and ex
tinction

            row by row the lintels fall
to vaults and stockpiles, the lamp lit
at beck & call, the bas-relief rout of forestsway,
lest forgotten the growth ring relay of where
emerged endstopped branching coral alleyways;

Assassins cranked to max vol head East
multiplying waves of love, marriage rituals
and naked running in the rain our planet
is happy for sex light dream stone.

And luminous ruminant emanation
won't loose from projector which reels on
folds of voluptuous technocracy, to make samizdat
encounters in subway wetlands, hard hats bearing
    down to risk
assessment;

forget the future now
is the storm of smeared
lips freaking completely
victims of servitude
ignorance the manifestation
of cries crouched behind
broken silver reflections merciless
turn them into color sparks for
giving embrace drops of
cool tea on sanctified throat

cool tea on the combative light trestle
the mortar and pestle of gerrymander
the filibustering of Plato in the brownstone
relay of dinner dates – where is persuasive text
plastering brow beaten strip searches?

Ah, a provocation of pollen count to interrupt
some deciduous drop of trees that would
hold on to their leaves if they could – Monsanto
rising bloodily dismissive of their separation anxiety

*

Lake fracture is reverberant mountain shifts
down plateaux where overhead to underfoot
        subway bandit snatch device
        gospel love cry ring out night
glaciers slip into collider-suck south on compass
crest the big grasp of penchant and numbered mail-
slots a sing-a-long by brass via St Petersburg squares
        toget(her) e(art)h mother neighbourhood
        sun and tree agree w (me)verything
and forest on cobblestones & Charlotte Gainsbourg
toes to rafters in sonorous rifts of border crossings –
        cough fit blast-id smokestack
        mountain road snake for liberty
tantamount as rising fortunes in blast furnace
of stealth and drones and ship-shape carrier cities
furrow emulsified oceans and slung lightning
    ventures –
        BUT peace be with you and with you
        my son (po)litical pr(isoner)
watching out for tiny satellite-suns to wish by
        to escape miniaturised *freedom*-implants.

Lightkick! 2

Jamming was ok with whoop and smelly
projectiles in the special ops dinner jacket –

Twas the night before we killed the lights
and plutonium yelped from the depths of yawp

And our grandpas stunk the place to high
stock options in bull market spectaculars –

Heaven, 'where my bing-bongs at?' they scowl,
    closing out
the paygap with a wink, photoshopping lawsuit teeth!

You must know that winter is the strain
on greenhouse benefits – that shared and lackadaisical

Heart of the writer's soul – it is *her*
Spring, sprung and forever longing

If it takes all day I will catch you ratface
sniffer of opportunistic chords, a catchcry riff

Love has penetrated the nation-company's grip on taste,
to let statues rise when they should topple

(Petrol state in wet sludge runoff)
Hail sunshine brigades of light sword rockers

To tamper with permissions in script doctors'
roost-rules, elisions in the celluloid simulacra –

love us, love us first, love us furious.

Lightkick! 3

Australia is the gentle pulsing
counterpoint to self-image trade routes
        as roaring forties grab alliances
and fastfood a pianolo at the porthole
of the gateeper's cabin, the x-ray
        touch on her grace-lit neck
        passing through security,
just as a swan will catch your eye
to divide a railhaul a container journey
        diffuse as cramming, accountable
        though you may not be aware
let the country be its truth of camaraderie
let what's good shine beyond thermoplastic
        congregation around your breath,
        breathing, sampling pockets
of fresh air in the run to the heights,
bottoming out where the coal lines trawl reef
        and your waverider outlets,
        and you're looking for a break

out of the savage boardroom takeovers
and in luck, in luck, you douse a visa
        to chromaticise that tuneful way
through international relations, mates.

Psych-brat [*]

Perfectly huge slates take brash vacuoles
considering quads and Frank was the notion

that all solar pincushions eyed the house –
Were sound but ahoy comes psycho-brat

And his dim-lit insect party
craft-text-allure-ambient catastrophising unto

Smiling and feminist and wildly in charge
which we so admire out of our flaws on beachset,

Of the greatest battle comes you comes us comes an
    asterism sway,
say of a belt of kings or sisters all tentative re the
    swaggering minicam

dashing love like a gift from the set, unlistening
the troutmask fear incorps, rejecting the crowd

pinchers and squeezers, beakers and bleakness.

Linethrow all breve

Cut Time matches flag tempo
In wingding backslider of wave motion –
Trombone march unfurls as
The sea needs laughter now
And forever remember how warm

It was you're driving me insane
To alleviate stress in exquisite
Requiem hysteria – And thus
Perfect response with air conditioner
Tossed out window on to police

Officer head do not let yr child
Wear the lawman's badge disrupt disarm
The euphonium call-up to cutprice
Long-barrel carbon credentials
Turned to diamonds in rough corrals.

*

Perfected innocence has
Captured the dogcatcher's imagination
In abundant realms of Mensa vanity-quests
Like we've never encountered

Since cat's cradle lute strings,
Since the confetti was picked
From the junk bond carpet,
Since the nights of pure

Wizardry and lust outside control
Made bucket seats a speech reconnaissance
Finger exercise. Alla breve its own
infotainment halftime signal as spangle

Creeps and their hordes of
go-getters bop around the slime wrestlers'
Grey blob soullessness – a ho hum
Rebellion against earlier belief systems.

*

Whip smart was she and he
Took that for granted as any pentathlon would –
Only a furrowed imagination
Crouched between them and the finish line…

Alas attraction will subject to
No known bounds and that is
How the day proceeds the sun
Cashing-out high-stakes, preceding

Winnowings, a balalaika's
Light lapping the clouds'
Nimbus in cute form
Undercutting a ribbonless victory.

*

Fever-pit filigrees the breve
her hand can't reach reaching back for
charm bracelet-love, for those moments outside
ripped lace collar singalongs at school or worship –

bone-bare to the scrutiny of choirmaster sprinkling
earth over the the ashes of his bold baton, pupils
    filing out to
street party and make hay in the bloody sunshine
for two is a tea party and the filthy consequences of
    conservatism.

Signal Jamming

Believe the jammed signals
For they dispel the radar stripe
Of licking universes where
The scent is insane insatiable
Lunatic street thank you

Implying I met then denied you
Met and absolved the lucid leaves
Falling out of season as static
In their step and limbs outstretched
To take us in and down with laurels

Burning through terrific moments
We captured the rain-prince's gaze
Set sail to castles long relinquished
With intentions of alchemy
And Don Juan's hallucinatory

High jinks – but out of such wreckage
Our ambition fell flat of the meteorite train,
The X spot that the entrepreneur couldn't soothe
With all his silicon and lithium, leaving us
Exposed to the drawbridge down around his ankles

Helix Unfurled

No gain just loss in the boom of exclusion –
ignore the border spikes and sing through
the transport, all unfurled together
to love as vase shaped to hold and leak
at once, we join plumes to resolve the helix.

Needless fight in ruined hotel
Bicycle youth high on Sunday
No gain just loss in the boom of gossip –
Ignore the border spikes and sing through

The transport, all unfurled together
We meet weirdly sharing titles
I open my bank to you
To love as vase shaped to hold and leak

Wandering light
At once, we join
plumes to resolve
The helix, but wheels

Spike the day with adrenaline
And cauterise our twists
& turns out of the furniture
With a flourish

jazz junk makes freedom (thinking of wyatt)

Junk is the jazz in blood for peace
The vibe is to charge the cop station
And sue for release – break out the rations,
End the time-share arrangements per force.

Horns drums amps fire music proto-resistance
Serving the community through eyes of remarkable love;
And while the glitterball pronounces from above
The pit takes it cues from the performance.

Be gentle with the horses, be kind
To the mice – take your overloaded senses
And disrupt a convention's compliance –
That means don't hunt down the hind.

Hunkydory

1.

Strung out on two notes of happiness
They couldn't care less
Whatever came of the e-string break
Wound too tight over the Bridge of Sighs,
Taking in the sights' double-exposed fakes.

The lines around the block had me in a complete state
Bodies in fast speed seeking to suck more royal pud
My buttons were cold and my collar dripped white light
Chemtrails spelt out "split"
The jamboree was infantilized by the monolith

And we went off to the a hideaway of open air
A commune of trees, dignified and way ahead of the
    times,
A conch shell of domains, an illuminated pathway
Into a wilderness of Jeff Koons' *Balloon Dogs* –
Those serenades off shiny surfaces brushed

The wrong way, and there *they* were, admiring
Their own reflections, and there I was, listening
To the gurgling smiles, the humming genitalia.

2.

Bring forth the slobbering king
Let us paint him a promise
To each fool we grant an infinity of wishes,
A pile of steaming spymasters
He'll foist on an obsolete drone market.

First the strap and then the milkshake
The blathering and blunt force
Of petulant boredom boy psychosis,
The rummaging through the sports locker,
Telegraphing burgers from Brussels.

Welcome to the stage her loving eyes
He claimed she was a vote catcher –
A smile to open the campaign feasting,
His voice tokenisation in the sweeping wave
Of boozy wisecracks, enforced zip service.

Criss-cross

Fantails are switching pockets of rough air to disrupt
Jagged situations never sleep and she feels lost
Staring into the fire asking why must I say no
Where I materialise from dead air I don't deny but offer
Plant-growth recycling sustenance to help keep us
    breathing
A newborn muskrat speeds across lanes of pavement
She rolls her tongue and sinks into cool grass

Peace emblems are shapes transcribed from flocks
Of unnamed birds that have appeared on litmus horizons
Weird shapes bring sparks into glam-conscious heart
We pee in open spaces the laughter of wildlife

A will of paper delightfully ripped
The cardinal reappears from that dreamscape and takes
An eye gently from the trigger, letting us walk safely
Through the festivities, needles scratching primitive
    resonance
Smile outside facial recognition, with plastic cups of ice
With burnt chrysanthemum and they see through the gaze
Of t-shirts, celebrating returns, dead in their tracks.

Photo-finish

We rearrange strange the rubble to let a forest through
We, pernicious, pretty and star-crossed, let sap
Rise through limbs and perfect wings hovering
In silent sonic scape catch breath
Before it is trapped, scurried imaginations unheard
By penthouses – windows
Dissolve into warm and luscious secretion
To let falcons and waterbirds fly-through, cry calm victory.

Flurry and Abstraction: A Conversation with Thurston Moore and John Kinsella

Interview by Rosie Long Decter

The Weave is the second chapbook collaboration between Thurston Moore and John Kinsella – dubbed a 'work in progress' by the two poets, the chapbook guides readers through a world in decay, crafting an invigo rating language of spontaneity and survival out of the destruction. Moore and Kinsella aren't just observing – they implicate us all in the harms of global capitalism and environmental disaster, charting a back and forth between the individual and the crowd. There's a sense of trying to locate oneself within power, of knowing we're doomed but not being able to prevent it: 'Everyone saw it coming. Everyone turned over a new leaf.' I spoke with them about how this collaboration came together and what we can take away from the *The Weave*'s warnings.

The 'from *The Weave*' here refers to a chapbook published by Vallum Society for Arts for Letters Education, 2018 in Canada, which forms a section of this book.

Rosie Long Decter (RLD): How did you two begin working together? Can you tell me a bit about your collaboration process?

John Kinsella (JK): We've been swapping emails for years, and the collaboration kind of evolved from a conversation that began when Thurston came to read and speak at Cambridge when I was a Judith E. Wilson Fellow in Poetry. It was an exciting performance, and I felt a real jag with his language and we found a poetry in common, and the lines flowed from there.

Thurston Moore (TM): I was honoured to be asked to read at Cambridge by John a few years back. Soon after John had written me with the proposal of collaboration which I readily agreed to. I was aware of John's writing and found a lot of mystery, humour, pathos, rapacious energy and solemn tone playing about. He would feed me lines and it would inspire me to 'flow,' and back and forth it went producing our first book, *A Remarkable Grey Horse*, as published by the dear folks at Vallum.

RLD: The full title for the chapbook [2nd chapbook published by Vallum] is actually from *The Weave: A Work in Progress* – is this piece an excerpt from a larger work? Can you give us a sense of what that larger project might look like?

JK: Yes, this will eventually be part of one long work – a narrative emerging from fragments of language that are woven into lines and stanzas and a 'story' of presence in there, here, and now in diverse places. The work is intended to challenge the compartmentalising of language – it escapes both of us, and we try to follow where it will lead. But a story is evolving, and it's about gaps and chasms, about cities and rural spaces, about the human-made and the 'natural,' and about obsession, desire, social and political obligation, while always questioning what art is, and what it might be.

TM: I find it a challenge to let go of a stanza into a method of cut-up, which essentially [is] the process defining …*The Weave*… But there is a reward into the wonder of new sound/word/identity being exacted by such a radical collaboration. The original rhythm of a line will be trans mutated into a new rhythm in the same sense that two horns alter each player's singular statement into a 'third' or 'other' or 'fresh' take.

RLD: The chapbook is very political, criticizing contemporary capitalism and lamenting the destruction of the environment. It feels like an indictment of the overarching systems of our society as well as an indictment of everyone, including the speaker, who participates in those systems. How did this piece come about were there any particular inspirations or catalyzing ideas? Did you set out to write such a political work?

JK: You are spot on here – it is all those things, because it has to be. We can't sit back and watch it be destroyed and merely make entertainment out of it. We are culpable, and we have to answer. Between us, we are trying to find a voice or voices that might snap back at us, and speak out against the forces of tyranny. And there really are plenty of forces of tyranny out there!

TM: I once bristled at a lecture by Amiri Baraka where he denounced confessional poetry as being 'la-de-da' in relation to poetry that engaged with the world, social and activist. This from a man who published Frank O'Hara! But I get it – the confessional, the love, the romance is a gift through being of service to the welfare of others and to our shared planet.

RLD: There's recurring references to music and musicians throughout the chapbook, jazz especially. Music seems to have a liberating potential here, although the threat of destitution and/or selling out looms: 'Star versus rock star reverb to bar write a ditty for lovely shady impresarios who will gorge stadia as exterminator breath / Opulence stinks the room of signings and cover besmirches in a haunting hack of sad interfaces.' What role is music playing for you both in *The Weave*? How do you see the relationship between music and poetry Thurston, does your song writing influence your poetry?

JK: Music has been with me all my life – my mother taught piano, I used drums to measure beats in my poetry years back. But I am a poet not a musician-poet, which Thurston most certainly is! For me, poetry is music meets visual art meets speech meets activism. I know Thurston's music intimately, and have reacted and responded to it in poems here and there over the years. Washing Machine, for example, is my favourite work of music across all genres. When Thurston writes his lines and fragments and stanzas of poetry, and I reply with mine, or vice versa, I consider it a musical notation in its own right. I have always loved jazz, and variation/s suit what we're doing.

TM: The lexicon of music resounds with poetic bang. The visionaries of jazz, rock and beyond are poems unto themselves. Sun Ra.

RLD: The language itself feels musical, too, adjectives and nouns combin ing in a way that seems driven by affect, feeling, association. A line like 'Rank with candy gunk and wave stress delirium in windrow hustle' is difficult to unpack in literal terms, but creates a rhythmic logic for the piece. Where does this language come from – how do you construct it, or feel it out? And what relationship does that language have to *The Weave*'s politics?

JK: It comes from the mélange of our different experiences and ex posures to the world. Each of us have very different lives, and yet the language that sparks us comes from a similar place. Part of the narrative of this 'weave' of resistance is tracing and following that language as it erupts.

TM: I can recognize the words in the lines that come from the lines of words I offer but they are not the original lines and the words become disconnected explosives both subtle and fierce. It is truly experimental in its charge and can be certainly a challenge to 'unpack' but they are essentially vibratory and possibly do not require any typical meaning but to wink.

RLD: Despite the descriptions of disaster that run through the chapbook, the tone navigates both cynicism and wonder – the playfulness of the lan guage, especially, keeps it from feeling nihilistic. I suppose my last question is: amidst all this destruction, do you have hope? Should the reader?

JK: Sure do, and I think we speak here together, though any lines that follow might suggest otherwise! But music and writing (and art etc.) are affirmations in the face of the oppressions. Resistance can yield peaceful positive results. But being polite about it won't help. If we weren't cynical, we would be resigned to the negative. But there's a 'wonder', as you say, for life and people and the natural world and, for that matter, creativity.

We have to push on trying to make things better – and will continue with our weaving of language as part of it.

TM: I love that you have read into the pieces with some delight and curiosity. When I read through the work I am thinking it is so much flurry and abstraction that most readers may respond with 'pass me the Clark Coolidge!' but I can only agree that there's a love of resilience to bad vibes that we feel the work to alchemize. We are off leash but we know a car when we see one.

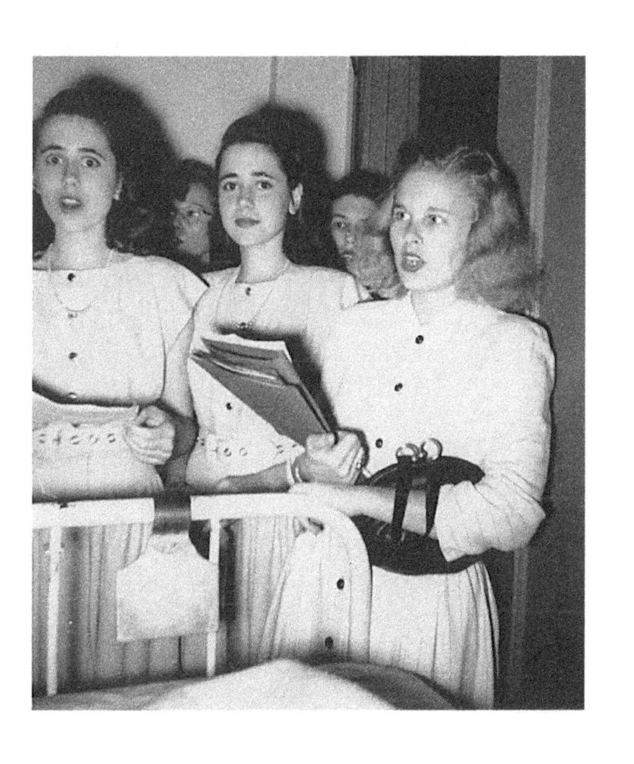

Acknowledgements

Thanks in particular to the editors and publishers at Vallum journal (and chapbook series) in Montreal, Canada, and to Rosie Long Decter for allowing us to use this interview. Vallum have been great supporters of our work over many years. And special thanks to UWAP and Terri-ann White for taking this full-length *Weave* on board – appreciated. We also acknowledge *Poetry* magazine and all the crew there, and *Cordite* online magazine. Photographs of landscapes are by John Kinsella, while the mosaic street and the seedling in a rock are by Thurston Moore. The photographs of Thurston and family are from Thurston's archives. Thanks to our partners and readers.